Have fun!

Donna x :)

signed edition

Words
Can
Fly

I dedicate this book to every child who has ever checked under their beds for monsters. After many, many years, I can confirm I've never found one. What a thing! – **D.A.**

To my parents, whose unwavering love and strength ignite the fire in my belly. I dedicate this book, and all of my achievements, to you. – **E.M.**

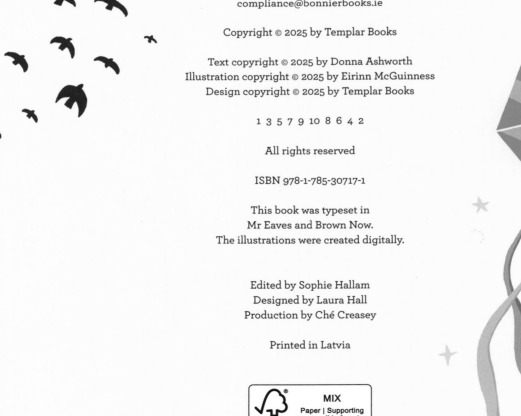

A TEMPLAR BOOK

First published in the UK in 2025 by Templar Books, an imprint of Bonnier Books UK

5th Floor, HYLO, 105 Bunhill Row, London, EC1Y 8LZ
The authorised representative in the EEA is Bonnier Books UK (Ireland) Limited. Registered office address: Floor 3, Block 3, Miesian Plaza, Dublin 2, D02 Y754, Ireland
compliance@bonnierbooks.ie

ISBN 978-1-785-30717-1

This book was typeset in
Mr Eaves and Brown Now.
The illustrations were created digitally.

Edited by Sophie Hallam
Designed by Laura Hall
Production by Ché Creasey

Printed in Latvia

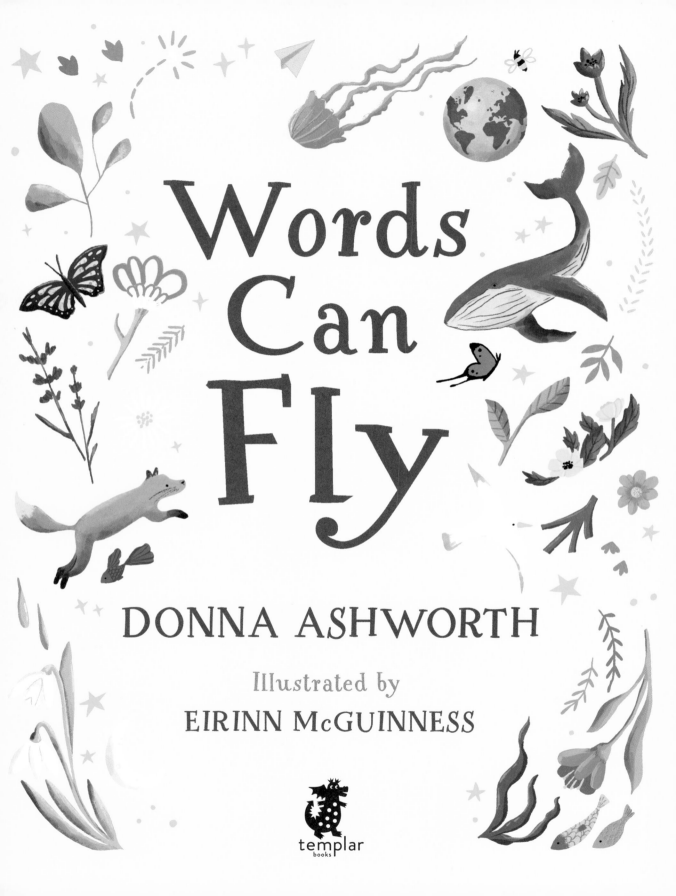

Words Can Fly

DONNA ASHWORTH

Illustrated by

EIRINN McGUINNESS

templar
books

CONTENTS

Welcome into this book...

where everyone is welcome and all feelings are accepted, just as they are.

Join Dave, Brian (the dogs), Sheldon, Mani (the cats), Benny (the bearded dragon) and me, as we remind one another that life is a pick-and-mix of all things – and that kindness and love make everything just that little bit better.

I like choosing a random page every day . . . somehow, the message always seems to fit. Perhaps for you or a friend? What is the poem trying to tell you? How does it make you feel?

No matter what, it's all perfectly imperfectly okay. Poetry isn't just for school – it's the sharing of thoughts you can't *quite* find the words for, or finding new ways to tell people how you feel. It's a way through the noise of a busy brain into a more peaceful place. And it can be fun too . . .

Come on in, and take your fill
this book requires your part
if you're wondering where to go
then this page is the start

let all your troubles flee your mind
let fresh words fill your head
the only way to be is kind
you'll see, once you have read

so take a seat and cosy in
the time is ticking by
sit down and let the pages show
that words can really fly

Messy threads

A poem is a messy thread
you pull out from your brain
and use to stitch a picture
to make some sense again

you take the thoughts all jumbled up
and sew them into lines
until your stitches make a shape
and you're left feeling fine

and if you read a poem
that someone else has sewn
the pattern might be quite like yours
and you'd feel less alone

so pull those messy threads out
and weave them into art
and you'll be left with tidy brains
with space for thoughts to start.

Talking

It is always good to talk
about the worries in our head
or the fears we feel at night
of monsters hiding under beds

talking is the light that shines
through the foggy night
bringing comfort to our minds
seeing everything's alright

and sometimes words are tricky
when the feelings aren't so clear
but just begin, your words will win
and find somebody's ear

start with saying *I feel*
or *do you ever wonder?*
and watch them go, the words will flow
like rain that follows thunder

keeping them in inside
I think would be a flop
they'll fizz like bubbles in a drink
one big shake, and they will **POP!**

Fitting

Puzzle pieces have to fit
to make a picture
but you can stand out if you like . . .
because humans are not puzzle pieces

we make a whole picture by ourselves
we mustn't change to be like someone else

if everyone did that
we would be left with just one picture
when we could have so many more

all colours, all sizes
all being free with no disguises

puzzle pieces have to fit
to make a picture
but the only time you have to fit
is when you're playing hide and seek.

Butter side down

If you drop your toast at breakfast
and that toast falls to the ground
why does it always land
butter side down?

the science will say
it is all kinds of things
like gravity and how
a falling object likes to spin

but I think it's because
some days are just that way
like traffic lights and stop signs
getting in your way

like soggy socks, rainy days
and playtimes spent inside
when all you want to do
is go out and seek and hide

oh, silly me, hide and seek
that's what I meant to say
maybe I'm just having
a butter-side-down day.

BUS
STOP

Youier

Imagine if the moon refused to shine
because the sun was shinier

if streams ceased to flow
because the rivers were flowier

if snow didn't dare to fall
because rain was fallier

if planets did not glow
because stars were glowier

if tigers did not roar
because lions were roarier

if flowers didn't flower
because their neighbours were flowerier

if a breeze didn't blow
because the gale was blowier

and trees did not branch
because the forest was branchier

what a world it would be if nature compared

you, my friend, must stop all that

no one can be more you
you are **youier**.

Why you are youier

No one sings just like you
no one thinks just like you
likes the same amount of water
in their drink, just like you

no one laughs just like you
plays in the bath just like you
walks across the lines along
the garden path, just like you

no one grows just like you
picks their nose just like you
no one runs, or jumps, or bats, or balls
or throws, just like you

you're the best at being you
if they could test what you do
there's no other in this world
who could contest, *that's the truth.*

Exercising kindness

Kindness is like any sport
practise makes you better
just like standing in the rain
for longer, gets you wetter

kindness is an energy
it feeds upon itself
and slowly trickles down
like honey spilt upon a shelf

and kindness is contagious
there is a magic in its hue
if you do something for someone
chances are they'll do that too

sometimes it's not so easy
when the world feels quite unkind
to find that goodness in your heart
and bring it to your mind

but when you do, you will be glad
as sparkles fill the air
and a smile lights up a cloudy face
from their mouth up to their hair

yes kindness is like exercise
it builds your kindness core
and the *joy* you get from happy friends
makes you want to do it **MORE!**

Phones and brains

Though I have an android
and you an iPhone
we can still talk to each other
as soon as we get home

and though one uses software
that's different from the other
we can watch our favourite things
without an ounce of bother

our brains are like that too
they don't always wire the same
but we can still connect
to enjoy our favourite games

learning to adapt
to the differences we see
is part of being human
and it helps both you and me

What is happy?

If happy was a colour
I think it would be yellow
golden, light and bright
a shiny little fellow

if happy was a taste
I think it would be sweet
and if it had a smell
it would not be stinky feet

no, I think it would be cake
or fish and chips outside
waiting at the fair
for a rollercoaster ride

if happy was a place
it would be my bed at night
tucked up safe and warm
with my toys there by my side

and happy feels like friends
coming to my house to play
on summer days with water guns
and homework out the way

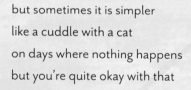

but sometimes it is simpler
like a cuddle with a cat
on days where nothing happens
but you're quite okay with that

happy is a feeling
and I know it when it's here
because everything feels yellow
and I smile from ear to ear.

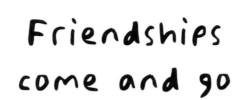

Friendships come and go

I don't know why it happens
but some friendships fizzle out
even though there was no argument
to fizzle out about

I don't know why it happens
but some friendships fade away
leaving memories and confusion
and wishing we could play

I don't know why it happens
but some friendships do not last
and all the fun and laughter
becomes a memory in our past

I don't know why it happens
but I know that it's okay
they come and go but you must know
that some will come and stay

and the ones that stay are gifts
they are sunshine through the cloud
if one's all you've got, it's a lot
you should be very proud

because friendships are like star-drops
we just catch when magic's near
some you must let go but some will grow
with strength from year to year.

Have you ever planted a seed
and watched a brand new flower rise?
Wow, you've been doing that
since the day you opened your eyes.

Pets

Pets have little lives
but they live them BIG
they play BIG
they eat BIG
they love BIG

but they only stay
for a small amount of time

so we must treat every day with our pets
as BIG-ly as they do

and love them BIG too

they're a small part of our lives
but their whole life is *you*.

Chocolate

It's hard to be someone
whom everyone likes
I am not even sure
it is possible

for example, I heard
that some people
don't like chocolate

and if chocolate itself
cannot please the whole world
then I think perhaps
neither can we

but when people *do* like chocolate
they really like it an awful lot

they save their money to buy it
and share it with their best friends
and favourite family
(but never pets!)

and when they eat it
they close their eyes
smile, as though they're thinking
lovely thoughts

and feel very wonderful
for just a short moment in time
in this busy, crazy life

so, I suppose
what I'm trying to say is
you can't be liked by everyone

but to some

you can be chocolate.

Positive thinking

Positive thinking

is not pretending
bad things don't happen

it is deciding to imagine
the good things happening instead

and using hope
like a magic wand
to make that good come true

positive thinking
is deciding not to waste
your brilliant imagination
on worrying

but using it instead

to create all the most
glitteringly fabulously positive things
you can find

within your
spectacularly, mightily mighty
magic-making mind.

Sleepy heads of spring

Spring feels like jumping
into a swimming pool and waking up
after a long, sound slumber. Everything is fresh
and new and coming back to life. Even us. Light is
creeping in around every corner and the air just feels full of
promise, excitement and new beginnings. Look around you in
springtime and take heed of the gardens and forests. It is time
to rise, time to stretch and grow taller, like the buds sprouting
from the earth. It is time to be hopeful and light, to get excited
about what is ahead. Life is happening, all around us.
Wake up sleepy heads, spring says, *let's grow*.
We have much to be brighter for.

Pineapple pizza

If you ask for pineapple on a pizza
someone, somewhere will say *ewww*
we can all agree this fruity fact
is a universal truth

and that could make you think
that your taste in food and drinks
is not as normal as everyone else
but so much food would be left on the shelf

if everyone said *gross*
and no one chose the cherry sauce
or drank the guava and dragonfruit flavour
and everyone just wanted Quavers

what would pineapples think
if they could only be chewed
or drunk in a drink?

let the pineapples have their day
let them be eaten in the most delicious of ways
with cheese and tomato on a pizza base
for that pineapple-pizza-loving face.

Our lights

I think everyone has a light

it isn't sparked by our cleverness
or the awards upon our shelf
it fires from deep down inside of us
somewhere we can't even see

and that light is all our own
no one can take it away
unless we let them

when we walk into a room
it is our light that people see
without even realising

and it is that light that draws in friends
who like the way our particular light shines
it's not that it is better than any other light
it is just the kind of light
their light is drawn to

if we hide that light of ours
because someone said it was too shiny
or not shiny enough
the people who would like it
would not see it
and they may walk right past
never even knowing it was there

so let your light shine out

even on days when we don't feel bright
that light of ours still twinkles
the only thing that can switch it off
is believing it is not good enough
no light can survive that fate

our lights remain bright with approval

not approval from anyone else
but simply approval from ourselves.

Snow in summer

Sometimes I am sad

even when the weather is sunny
and my eggs are perfectly runny
and my baby brother just did
something really quite funny

sometimes I am sad without reason
like snow falling in the summer season
like a scratchy cat who has no fleas on

it makes no sense

but I think maybe that's the clue
that sadness can just visit you
doing something as normal
as lacing a shoe, it's true

and when sadness visits, I just let it
hang around, I don't upset it

because everybody knows
without rain, no flowers grow
sadness comes and sadness goes.

Over rainbow bridge

My pets are over rainbow bridge
they can't come out to play
they're busy living their best life
with the animal friends they've made

they run and run the whole day long
in fluffy clouds they sleep
they eat the grass that's made of cheese
and find more balls to keep

they're never lonely, never sad
they don't need to visit vets
they're happy all the hours long
what a life they live, my pets

my pets are over rainbow bridge
and though I miss them dearly
I think of them so light, so free
and feel their love so clearly.

Love

Love is all the kisses
planted on your head
when you are drifting off to sleep
and curled up safe in bed

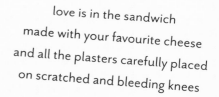

love is in the sandwich
made with your favourite cheese
and all the plasters carefully placed
on scratched and bleeding knees

love is asking *are you well
and did you eat your snack?*
it's in the water poured for you
to keep your health on track

love is in the yucky drinks
we sometimes have to swallow
to fill our bones with vitamins
so they are strong, not hollow

love does not land soft sometimes
it can be quite the shout
when cars are driving far too fast
and someone yells *watch out!*

yes, love comes in so many ways
you may not colour red
with hearts and hugs and kisses
love is sometimes shown, not said.

Blending

Families can be small or large
though all it takes is two
and families can be blood or choice
as long as they love you

a family can be one thing
and then something quite new
when people love more people
and you get to love them too

a family is not simple
because love is *everything*
so making sure your team is tight
can be a tricky thing

and all you need to know is
that nothing's black or white
there's every colour in our hearts
and blending those is nice

if you are mostly purple
and they are mostly blue
and dad is orange, mum is green
imagine all those hues

it can take some time to see
that blended rainbow in your pot
but when you do you'll realise
your family is **a lot**.

Step

Maybe you have
a stepsister or brother
a stepmum or a stepdad?

maybe that is fun for you
or perhaps it's sometimes sad?

maybe it's confusing
when birthdays come around
and you need to go between two homes
always moving round?

but think of it like this
a step can take you up
but you can turn
and go back down
and down again
or up

steps go in both directions
they're never just one-way
your life has just got bigger
and that's always pretty great

there are more people who love you
more people you can hug
more people to play games with
and care, when you've caught a bug

more people to like your artwork
more people means more laughs
these steps in life bring more to us
not less, just do the maths.

Middle

Some people always win
and some people lose a lot
and some people in the middle
think they don't matter a jot

if only they could see
this life's a shape-y riddle
and there's no shape without a bottom
and no shape without a middle

the tops of shapes are great
but bottom is quite vital
and middle is the filling
without a trophy or a title

sometimes you'll fall flat
and make the solid base
other times you'll reach the top
and win the race you grace

so just keep making shapes
and help others make theirs too
because wherever you have placed
is just a place . . . *it's not for good.*

Sometimes, we're never picked

for a game we'd like to play

but you know you can always start

your own game, anyway.

Your words

There are certain fine things
one must always say . . .
I like you
you're funny
and how are you today?

but as with most things
the opposite's true

here are some words
we should not hear from you . . .

I don't like your face
your hair is a mess
I hate your new shoes
why did you choose that dress?

when words reach your tongue
carry out a quick test
is it kind, is it helpful
is the message your best?

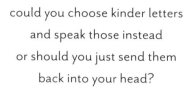

could you choose kinder letters
and speak those instead
or should you just send them
back into your head?

because words do a job
they deliver intent
so be careful to check
you said what you meant

and not what the monkey
who lives in your mind
spat out with some mischief
when he didn't feel kind

speak with much care
do you sound like you?
check on your words
are they kind, wise and true?

Constellations

Imagine if every single person who has ever cared about
you were to light up together in the night sky. Can you imagine it?
What a galaxy of stars that would be. Your twinkly constellation would be
brighter than Orion's Belt, the Plough *and* the Big Dipper. Imagine then,
adding in everyone you've ever been kind to, animals as well. What a star-bright
map the inside of your good heart would make. On days when you feel
a little dull, think of your sparkly night-sky constellations
of love, and let them light you up.

Grannies, Grans and Nans

Some people say **Granny**
and some may say **Gran**
some choose **Grandma**
and some may say **Nan**
but no matter the name
we all can agree
that **Gigis** and **Nannys**
are loved as can be
they always have time
to listen and play
and they never stop laughing
at the fun things we say
whatever they bake
it tastes super sweet
and hugging them
is the best part of my week
some people say Granny
and some may say Gran
no matter, we love them
as much as we can.

Grandads, Pops and Grandpas

Some people say **Grandad**
and some say **Grandpa**
some choose to say **Pops**
and some say **Granda**
whatever you call yours
I know you'll agree
that they are the best
if your kite's in a tree
or if there's a problem
you just can't work out
ask Grandad, he'll know
he'll be there in a shout
there's nothing in life
that your Pops won't make better
he'll teach you to fish
or to write a nice letter
some people say Granpaw
and some say Grandad
no matter, we love them
they make our hearts glad.

Signs

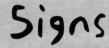

Have you ever seen a feather
softly floating from the sky
and watched your parents pick it up
then smile and happy cry?

it's because they feel these feathers
are signs from someone dear
someone we can no longer see
but our love keeps them quite near

and some people choose pennies
and see these as their sign
that angels in the heavens
are requesting them to shine

for some it's redbreast robins
who chirp a caring song
is it the song our loved ones sing
are these birds passing it on?

and rainbows drawn in colours
across the rain-drenched sky
are often someone's happy sign
that loved ones are close by

all these signs bring comfort
when we feel far apart
reminding us that love is all we need
to heal our heart.

Only

An only child suggests
that one is somehow *less*

but you are so much more
than *only*, you are ALL

and that is not small

you are EVERYTHING
not *only*

and if you ever feel lonely

remember how loved you are

you were wished for on a star
and it came true

along came you

more than enough for two.

you are EVERYTHING not only

Moving on

It's hard to leave a house
 that you've lived in for so long
 it feels like something's left behind
 that can't be brought along

the bricks, the walls, the roof, the drive
the garden, trees and path
can't be packed up in a box
and mostly neither can the bath

and though those things seem dear
as you lament what you can't take
it's really all the memories
these things have helped you make

and memories can be brought with you
they're light, they wrap up fine
the memories of fun water fights
and all those sunny times

you can also bring the cosy parts
the blankets and the throws
which wrapped you up on wintry days
and warmed your frozen toes

and love lives in the people
not the walls or rooms
the things you need are yours to bring
so let them light your gloom

it's hard to leave a house
that has felt like part of you
but home is where the heart is
and your heart is coming too.

Summer is funner

Summer is funner,
everyone can agree. The trees are
in full bloom and nature is riotous, colourful
and almost as ecstatic as leaving school for summer
holidays. Summer is ice-creams and late nights, where
even the sun doesn't seem to want to go to bed. It is life at
its most lifelike, summer. As though all the other seasons are
just preparing us to be here in this moment, running through
sprinklers and eating ice-cold watermelon. Picking daisies for
our hair, birds singing their encouragement as we play and
the feeling we could run and jump the entire summer day.
Summer is funner. And the only thing to do when
summer is upon you, is throw your hands up in
the air and jump in.

a friend for life when life gets hard

Siblings

If you are lucky enough to have a sibling
annoying you every day

stop for a moment and be glad
and yes I know they make you mad
when they call you silly names
or cheat to win a silly game

but one day
you will look at them and see . . .

a friend for life when life gets hard
someone to send a birthday card
or call when things are not so great
a sibling is a life-long mate

if you are lucky enough to have a sibling
annoying you every day

give them some sibling love
they are a gift from up above

(I said **love**, by the way, not **shove**!)

Words can fly

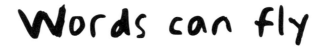

Did you know that words can fly?
allow me to explain
here is what those words can do
as they up and leave your brain

they trip down to your mouth
and jump right off your tongue
and float like little feathers
bringing comfort to someone

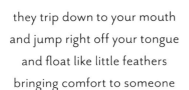

if the words you choose to speak
are funny, giggly ones
they will bounce into another's brain
and fill it full of fun

if the words you choose are kind
and not feelings run amok
they will fly into another's heart
and undo rusty locks

if the words you choose are mean
or hateful and unkind
they buzz like angry wasps
and sting the person's mind

and from that sting a seed will pop
and make a plant of sadness
that plant will find its power
from all the hate and badness

likewise, when the words are kind
they also bloom and grow
a flower of every colour
will take their root and glow

and maybe you can see with me
that garden in your mind
the field of flowers you're growing there
perhaps it's now the time . . .

to make sure all the seeds you cast
are seeds which will grow bright
the seeds that face the sunshine
and thrive on giving light

and whilst we're here, let me be clear . . .
when nasty seeds come in
you can flick them from your soil
before their growth begins

and cast them to the clouds
to disperse amongst the air
those seeds won't find a place to grow
just floating around there

keep your garden colourful
with plants of every kind
and help your friends grow their plants too
in the gardens of the mind.

Faults

If someone calls you a name
or tells you that something you like
or something you do
is silly . . .

it is easy to think
that this must be true
that something must be
very wrong, inside you
but no, the problem
is not what you do
it is all in the heart of
who's looking at you

the person who said this
is not seeing you
they are seeing a mirror
reflecting their truth
so let them say what
they feel they must say
you will go on being you
as you do every day
true to your heart
in each possible way
knowing kindness
won't look
for faults
anyway.

Raincloud

There will be days when it feels as though no one
wants to choose you, or play with you, or ask you around to tea. Days when nothing
seems to go right and your heart feels heavy. We all have them. Days when it feels
as though we have our own personal raincloud following us around, squeezing cold water
on our heads. But the thing is, that raincloud will dry up, as all rainclouds must. The sun
will eventually come out, that's a fact, and a little rainbow might just stretch out from
your cloud's marshmallow middle, filling the air around you with colour and joy, if you let it.
So yes, you may have your own little grey raincloud, following you around some days,
but you could also have your own rainbow too. Think about
that for a moment . . . there it is.

Ordinary

Extraordinary things are wonderful
like fireworks on bonfire night
but have you ever found a stone
that had perfect shiny stripes?

or had a butterfly land
upon your shoulder blade
whilst the sun twinkled through the trees
as you played within their shade?

what about the taste
of ice-cream in the sun
or hot chocolate when it's cold and grey
and you're inside having fun?

the little things in life
are often overlooked
but if we peer with seeing eyes
we may find our senses shook

for ladybirds are magical
and birds sing like Taylor Swift
bubbling streams for paddling feet
are nature's little gifts

so yes, life has its big stuff
and those things can blow our minds
but don't forget to search the small
there's much magic you can find.

Planet prayer

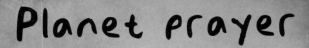

Everything that makes this world
exists inside of you
we each are born of atoms
we are all just passing through

a star is full of elements
and you are built the same
just slightly rearranged
moulded in a different way

this planet spins in place
a tiny speck just going around
yet we all stay upright
when the world turns upside down

so take a little moment
to wonder at this life
how magical the moon is
as it orchestrates the tides

and think of all the species
far too many kinds to name
relying on the atmosphere around
to stay the same

it is worth the extra work
to keep this planet cool
even if that means
walking back and forth to school

wearing clothes a second time
and turning off the lights
never wasting water
it is gold dust in our pipes

be kind to Mother Earth
she has taken so much strife
be careful with this planet
as you go about your life.

Hopetimism

Some people are optimists
some people are pessimists
and in the middle
sit the realists

optimists look
for the bright side of everything
pessimists look
for the worst that can happen
realists look at the facts

I am none of the above
perhaps you are like me?

I am a hopetimist
a mixture of all three of these things
but with hope added in

so perhaps I won't always see the bright side
but hope certainly stops me
from only seeing the worst
and when you mix hope with the facts
you get something quite lovely . . .

HOPETIMISM

facts, a little fear, and a whole lot of hope.

Fear

Fear can make us jump and shriek
when startled by the thunder
till we find our cosy blanket
to safely hide and cower under

fear is looking out of windows
high above the ground
our stomach loops a loop
like a crazy ride going round

fear can make us freeze
or even run quite strangely fast
but when the danger passes
fear moves on, it doesn't last

fear is there to keep us safe
and help us get away
from things that tried to eat us
back in olden days

but sometimes fear can linger
when there is no danger there
fear gets confused with what's unsafe
and what just makes us scared

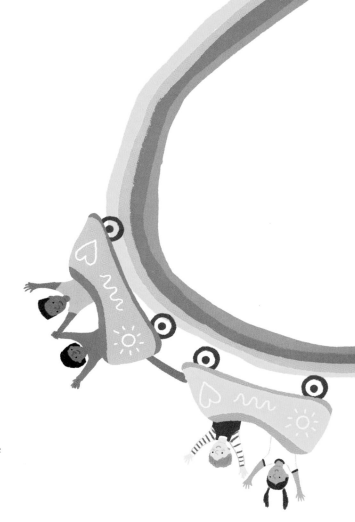

like homework we don't understand
or friends who cannot stay
like Mondays after weekends
we don't want to wish away

this fear can bring us worry
stop us living, hold us back
unless you learn to spot that fear
and stop it in its tracks

so be afraid of too-high heights
being hurt and falling down
but don't be afraid of failing
or letting teammates down

don't be afraid of joining in
or not being good enough
don't be scared to show your artwork
when your finish feels too rough

it's okay to fear the darkness
you can always flick the light
fear keeps us safely in one piece
but lets our brave shine bright.

Foundations

Most of our growth we cannot see

like a tree

with an underground web of roots
reaching deeper than its height is high
spreading out determined fingers
into the nurturing ground

yet all we see is the trunk above
and the branches and leaves it wears

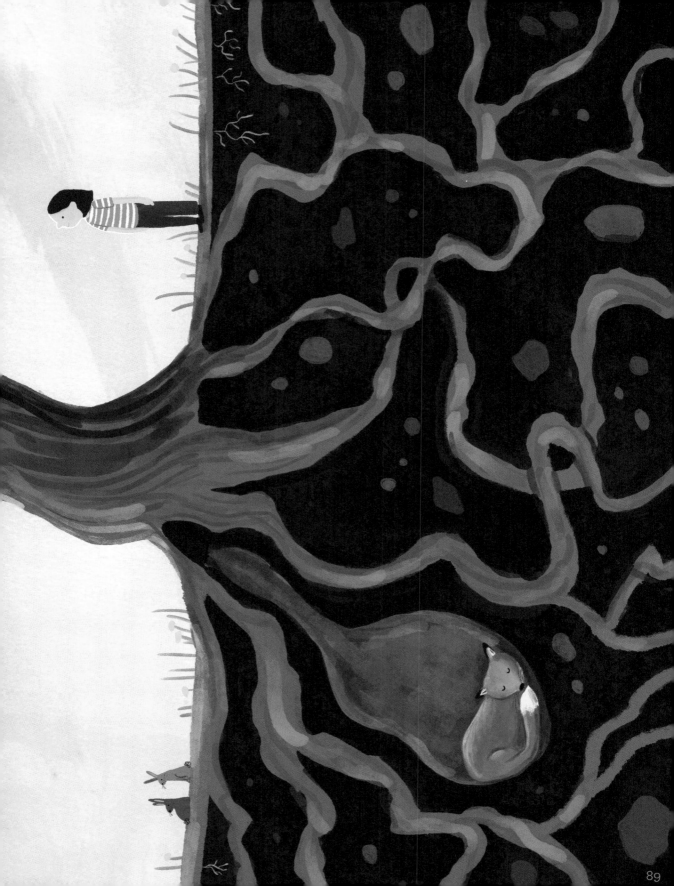

or the iceberg
floating brightly
its craggily icy peaks
a superior sight to behold
but nowhere near as majestically mighty
as the boundless base of it
cloaked by sea

most of who we are

cannot be seen

and the work we do

does not always show

but it is there

making us stronger

creating a steady base

so our leaves can bloom

our peaks can peak

and our foundations

will never be shaken.

Growing into school

The thing about big school
is that it's big, right?
and the thing about you
is that you're small, right?

but that won't always be so

each day you go to school
is a day you are growing
you can't always see it

it's not always showing

but it's always happening

and pretty soon
you will be big enough to see
that this school fits you
like bees fit their knees

so whilst it's still too large, remember . . .

each day that passes
is a day you're growing in
getting used to maps and rules
that once made your head spin

and please oh please
remember this too
that your friends and other fellows
feel exactly as you do

and whilst we are here
remembering, let us not forget . . .

that all these new faces
are just friends you haven't met

yet.

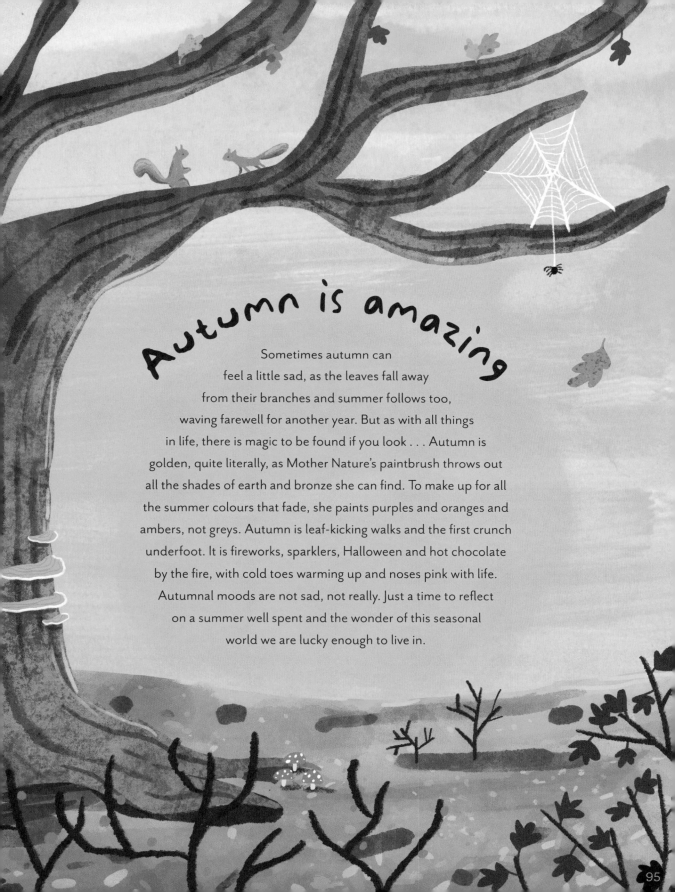

Autumn is amazing

Sometimes autumn can
feel a little sad, as the leaves fall away
from their branches and summer follows too,
waving farewell for another year. But as with all things
in life, there is magic to be found if you look . . . Autumn is
golden, quite literally, as Mother Nature's paintbrush throws out
all the shades of earth and bronze she can find. To make up for all
the summer colours that fade, she paints purples and oranges and
ambers, not greys. Autumn is leaf-kicking walks and the first crunch
underfoot. It is fireworks, sparklers, Halloween and hot chocolate
by the fire, with cold toes warming up and noses pink with life.
Autumnal moods are not sad, not really. Just a time to reflect
on a summer well spent and the wonder of this seasonal
world we are lucky enough to live in.

Voices

Do you sometimes hear
some little voices in your head
telling you to stay up late
to refuse to go to bed
telling you your drawing sucks
and isn't up to scratch
or telling you you're bad at football
right before a match?

are these voices kind and wise
or are they very naughty
are these voices on your side
or do they want to get you caughty
are they steering you to trouble
do they want to hear you shout
or are they all the things you've learned
just trying to get out?

pay attention to these voices
as you go about your day
work out if one is good
and one is leading you astray
tell them to pipe down
and speak up only when they're asked
and tell them you're the one in charge
when it comes to taking tasks

voices in our head are just
thought-monkeys in our minds
one is full of mischief
and the other very kind
so turn the nice one's volume up
and the other, turn him down
you don't need a naughty monkey
in your mind, making you frown.

Anxiety

Anxiety, oh my-ety
oh why, oh why, oh why-ety?

why do I feel so anxious
why is my heartbeat fast
why do I want to run and run
and run and run so fast?

anxiety, oh my-ety
oh why, oh why, oh why-ety?

where is my normal breathing
why won't it settle down
why are my hands all sweaty
my face a frozen frown?

anxiety, oh my-ety
oh why, oh why, oh why-ety?

place my thumb against my finger
and then the same, the other hand
place them on my eyes like glasses
concentrate on feeling calm

anxiety, oh my-ety
oh why, oh why, oh why-ety?

now breathe it in and count to three
breathe out and count to four
focus hard on something simple
like the window or the door

anxiety, oh my-ety
oh why, oh why, oh why-ety?

now start to hear your heartbeat
slowing like a storm
that's running out of rain
making way for sun so warm

anxiety, oh my-ety
oh why, oh why, oh why-ety?

release the anxious bubbles
crashing crazily round your chest
make space and fill with breathing
that soothes your mind to rest

anxiety, oh my-ety
goodbye, goodbye, goodby-ety!!!

Gratitude goggles

Have you ever had an eye test? Did the optician place goggles on your eyes and switch out the circular lens to make you see more sharply or less? I think about that when I am practising gratitude. My gratitude goggles, I call them . . . If I am feeling 'poor me' or have awoken with a thump and a strump, I try this first. On my goggles go, and quite like magic I look at everything differently. I have to make my bed? Isn't it great that my bed is so soft and my favourite stuffed panda is sitting there. Then, I start thinking about how funny giant pandas are, and how rare. And how great it is that I am alive at the same times as them, and off I go, being all grateful . . . it is quite magical. Try it. Pop on your gratitude goggles and see . . .

Joy

Joy is not the shiny toys
sat on a toy-shop shelf
it's the having friends to play with
when you've been all by yourself

it's the having family visit
bringing cuddles, treats and fun
it's running through the grass
laughing loudly with someone

joy is when your song
fills the radio in the car
and you're all singing along
even though you're not going far

joy won't stay all day
she pops in and out like sun
you can't keep her there for ever
she's supposed to go, and come

and when she does be ready
to smile and wave your hands
these moments wash away
just like your castles in the sand

but they leave a joyful memory
a star within your mind
and there's always pots of golden joy
in every day, to find.

S'Munday

At 4 o'clock each Sunday
I start to think of Monday
and the things I need to do
and the ways it makes me blue

and though Sundays are my fundays
I think they're spoiled by Mondays
creeping in before their time
pushing back their starting line

but listen, here's the thing
we must stop this happening
Sundays are a day of rest
we can't let them flee the nest

Monday has twenty-four hours
do not give it Sunday's power
do your spellings and your maths
then fizz some bubbles to your bath

splash and linger for an hour
go outside and smell the flowers
be protective of your Sunday
do not let it become S'Munday.

Screen time

Do you know that screen time
can happen in your mind?
when batteries run out
you can go there anytime

a good imagination
is like data never-ending
no need to download content
your brain is always sending

a world of wizards casting spells
why not, let's make that so
the spells are yours to shape
there's no one to tell you no

just pop inside your mind
when the iPads are offline
and see a world of wonder
you can access all the time

do you know that screen time
can happen without screens?
it's about the access to all things
and space where you can dream.

Rewrite

A lot of things happen in every day
and sometimes we get in each other's way
arguments blossom, from something quite small
it's hard to recall how it started at all

a lot of things happen in every day
emotions and tiredness can change what we say
and when we look back, we are sorry we chose
the words that we did, when our frustration rose

so all you can do, is let go, start again
apologise if you have upset a friend
and say something kind to rewrite what was drawn
tell them you care and your cross-ness has gone

a lot of things happen in every day
but don't let them linger or wander away
the people you know, are your people, you know
apologise, dry your eyes, come on, *let's go*.

Glad out of grumpy

Everyone wakes up grumpy sometimes, but the next time you do, remember . . . If you stay grumpy, everything around you will become grumpy too, it's true. Door handles will sharply poke you as you pass and pets will hiss and run away. Your friends might catch your grumpy from you, and before you know it your teacher will have it and the whole world will be in a giant grumpy pickle. But if you break through the grumpy with gladness, remembering all the things you have to be pleased about (clue: they are everywhere), magic happens. Door handles open doors again and pets wag their tails when they see you. Friends will smile when your smile beams their way and the whole world will shimmer with a little extra shine, made just by you. And in a superbly powerful way, you can make glad out of grumpy.

Gratitude

Gratitude isn't about
saying thanks and please
that's just good manners
(and *I know* you have those)

being grateful is knowing
that the air in your lungs
is keeping you alive
and the food on your table
is not always on everyone else's

gratitude is seeing the people
who work around us every day
so we can do the things we like
and understanding how lucky we are
to have whatever it is we have
no matter how *simple* or *small*
because some people, somewhere
would think them *majestic* and *mighty*

gratitude is not just saying thank you
it is *being* thankful
for everything
because even the things
that don't seem so great
often bring lovely surprises
if we just gratefully wait.

About

It's not about your sea-blue eyes
or the curls within your hair
it matters not your shape or size
or the kind of clothes you wear

it's not about your clever traits
or the sports you like to play
it won't matter if you can't run fast
your life won't work that way

it matters if your words are kind
and your ears are listening in
it's all about your seeking mind
and the way you spread that grin

it matters if you tell the truth
and treat your friends with care
it's all about your loving heart
and those who'll nestle there

it's not about the tests you take
or the medals on your shelf
it's all about the thoughts you make
and the way you treat yourself

you cannot judge by looks, you see
or the things you have achieved
you only know the person
from the things you don't first see.

Everything in nature is growing
and remember, you are nature too
every day your growth is showing
in ways that only you can do.

Hope

Hope is the baby blackbird
sitting featherless in the nest
who watches and believes
he will fly like all the rest

it's the caterpillar climbing
into its dark cocoon
knowing he will come back out
much brighter, pretty soon

hope is the winter forest
bare of all its leaves
having dropped them to the ground
to wait for spring to breathe

it's the focused little spider
climbing up the water spout
who scales the pipe another time
despite being washed right out

hope is in our pockets
even though we didn't pay
it comes from giving up
then getting up, another day.

Wonderful Winter

Winter is wonderful.
Except, perhaps, for the dark mornings
that make it hard to get out of bed. And coming
home from school in darkness too, that can be tough. But
if you slow down just a little, like the nature outside, winter can
be magical. The twinkly lights that pop up everywhere in place of
the sun. The cosiness of sofas and candles smelling of cookies. Family
cuddles that seem to happen so much more; not to mention snow days,
frosty breath and crisp, cold mornings that feel warm somehow. Winter
feels warm, somehow. Perhaps because it is mostly celebrations, joy and
fun, and if it starts to get too cold, we can be like the trees and use
our ancient wisdom and patience. Don't fear. Light always comes
back, you see. Spring always comes again. And winter can be
wonderful, if you just cosy in, and let it.

Goodbyes

Goodbyes are never easy
that's something we all know
leaving someone's company
when you just don't want to go

or the ending of a party
when it's time to go to bed
but you haven't finished sharing
all the games within your head

and some goodbyes are harder
because there seems to be no *when*
we don't get to make another plan
to be with them again

and those goodbyes take time
to settle in our hearts
just hearing someone's name out loud
can cause fresh tears to start

and sometimes it can feel
as though they'll truly disappear
from your mind, with all its worry
it may seem hard to keep them near

but memories never fade
and your people live in those
you won't forget that laugh, or how
they wrinkled up their nose

the words they said will stay
and the stories that they told
live in your mind for all of time
even when you're old

so yes, goodbyes are hard
from that there's no escape
but all the things you loved in them
are yours, all yours, to take.

For tomorrow

I hope tomorrow is one of those days that feels like sunshine. A day when laughter is loud and the only tears are happy ones. Where schoolwork is easy, friends all agree and pets are extra cuddly. I hope today is chocolate-flavoured (or better still, chip-flavoured!) and full of things that bring smiles and fuzzy-covered dreams when you finally fall into a bed as soft as a cloud. I hope today is one of those days for you. But if it's not, do not fret. Simply pop today under your pillow when you curl up to sleep, and take all that hope and plant it there too. It may just grow overnight, using the mud of today as its soil, into a day full of sunshine for tomorrow.

Sadness

If sadness was a colour
I think it would be grey
murky, dull and flat
like a sunless rainy day

if sadness was a taste
I think it would be sour
but not like fizzy sweets
more like lemons dipped in flour

and the taste would make you feel
like you don't want to eat
and you don't want to play
with your friends out on the street

if sadness was a place
I think it'd be the park
but when everyone's gone home
and it's getting strangely dark

sadness can feel heavy
and as though it's just for you
it can make your world unsteady
it can make you feel quite blue

but the thing about this sadness is
it's often not that bad
it looks much worse than it truly is
in fact, it's often *glad*

because sadness comes from loving
if you're missing someone dear
sadness mostly comes from caring
that's why sadness comes with tears

sadness is the peak of mountains
of feelings we can store
when we probably should have freed them
making space for joy to soar

it's not trying to hurt you
or drain your life of fun
it could be there to hold a place
of a special lost someone

so do not fear when sadness swoops
to visit you again
you can ask it in and give it tea
and treat it like a friend

it won't outstay its welcome
it will take its leave quite soon
and you can open up your window
to let joy back in your room.

It is sadder to walk past
someone lost or all alone
than it is to be the one
sitting there all on your own.

Poetry is permission

As you open the pages
of a poetry book
you enter a mindset cocoon
a place where the thoughts
in your mind can be still
and your heart can take over the room

there are words here to spell
what you couldn't before
in each page you can lay down your fears
let the soothe of the words
warm the cold from your bones
use the rhyme to kiss dry any tears

there's no judgement in here
there's no right and no wrong
just others who've gone where you've been
you can rest here awhile
let the past slip away
let the poems describe what you've seen

as you open the pages
of a poetry book
you'll find refuge from life and its mission
you can unpack the bags
you've been dragging so long
you can *be*
poetry is permission.

For parents and carers

I hope you enjoy sharing the poems in this book with your little ones. These texts have been lovingly designed to spark thoughts and conversations, and unwrap topics which can often arrive entangled with confusion or fear. I have organised the themes for your ease when you need to find something specific, but I also recommend the random-page method . . . see what comes up and be open to the chats that ensue. These bonding moments of big-chats-disguised-as-an-ordinary-moment are the ones which may just stay lifelong. I can remember some myself. And the ones that don't feature as memories are nestled deep within our hearts, helping us stay kind and loving. What a thing.

For teachers

I would be delighted if you chose to use these poems in your lesson plans, particularly for emotional, social and mental wellbeing but also, of course, for practising language and poetry skills. For me, the best way to begin writing poetry is to think of a feeling and a topic and go from there. Am I trying to convey the scary feelings brought on by a big change? Then my emotion is fear and my topic is change. It's helpful to think of how these feelings may smell, taste or look if they were visible. Or if they were an animal, what would they be? I find that no subject is out of bounds with children when viewed through this simple lens, even grief. If grief were an animal to me, it would be a mysterious wolf that howls by the moon, alone in the dark of night. Scary if you don't realise that he is simply calling for friends who understand what he is feeling, and that in the morning the sun will be on his face and he will look fluffy and feel safe again. Even wolves need family, understanding and love.

I would love to hear how you have used the poems and what they brought about within your teaching worlds.

Dear reader,

You may use this book any way your heart wishes, but I love to choose a random page and see what the message is. If you are specifically seeking solace on a particular topic or hoping to cover a certain theme, this index will serve as a useful guide.

Love Donna

Poetry index

Emotions

Family

Change

Differences

Grief and loss

Mindset

Friendships

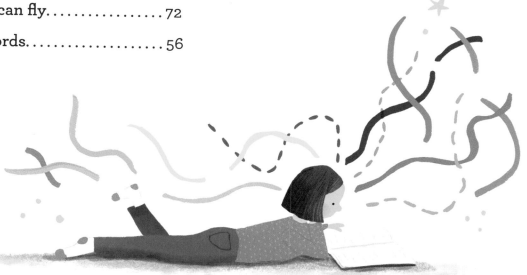

DONNA ASHWORTH

Donna Ashworth is a pet-loving poet who lives in the bonny hills of Scotland with her sons Felix and Brodie, her dogs Dave and Brian, her cats Sheldon and Mani (short for Maneki Neko, which is Japanese for 'lucky cat') and her bearded dragon Benny (who loves to shower every day!).

Donna has been writing poetry for adults since 2020, having published over ten poetry books, and finally decided it was time to create a book for children too.

'I'm a huge believer that magic is around us everywhere, if we just learn to see it . . . and who could be better at that than children? Life is so much more fun when we remember how to laugh, play, make friends and stop and talk to every animal we meet.'

Donna has almost two million followers across social media and would very much like it if you would follow her too, to see what the pets are up to and what wise words she has to share with you next . . .

EIRINN McGUINNESS

Eirinn McGuinness is an illustrator from Dorset, England, who can usually be found exploring the coastline with her sketchbook and surfboard. When Eirinn isn't scribbling or riding waves, she is also a primary school teacher who loves to share her passion for art, books and learning. She finds inspiration from the young people she works with and gets immense joy from watching her students grow.

Getting to bring Donna Ashworth's wonderful poems to life on the page was a very special experience, especially because *Words Can Fly* is Eirinn's first illustration project to be published. Now she can tell her students that your dreams are achievable, and chasing them is most definitely worthwhile!

A note from Donna

Thank you to YOU, who picked up this book and honoured it by reading the words and looking at the pictures. A book is only happy if it is read, so thank you for that joy.

Thank you to whomever bought or gifted this book because again, words can only fly if people let them . . . if they help them on their journeys from bookstores, through the skies and into hearts.

A HUGE thank you to the illustrator of this beautiful book, Eirinn McGuinness, who made everything come alive with her imaginative and heartwarming drawings and who captured my pets, Dave, Brian, Benny, Sheldon and Mani so perfectly!

Thank you to Lara Bruce (and her amazing mum Susanna, of course), for the expert help in your role as chief-child-editor. And to all the boys and girls at Lara's school, and to my sister Mrs Monteith and her class at Comely Park Primary School. Your suggestions and fun-filled ideas were so wonderfully inspiring (I especially loved the suggestion of pineapple pizza!).

And last but not least, thanks to Sophie and Laura, and my amazing team at Templar for all their joyful dedication and hard work. You are in the business of making magic and I am beyond thrilled to be a part of that with you.

Words can indeed fly, my friends.

What a thing

to sit back and watch!

Praise for Donna

'Donna's creativity with words is always impactful – and I'm so glad that now my children will be able to use her poetry in the way that I do. Brilliantly reflective, awakening and full of comfort. This is an offering of beauty.'

Giovanna Fletcher

'Beautiful and uplifting.'

Davina McCall

'A little corner of calm within life's storm – wonderful.'

Cat Deeley

'Like a warm hug, Donna's words are comfort for the soul.'

Tamzin Outhwaite

'So inspiring, so heartfelt… the way Donna writes is beyond beautiful.'

Lisa Snowdon

'Donna is a true wordsmith. Her writings never fail to move me.'

Nadia Sawalha